Original title:
Mystic Horizons

Copyright © 2024 Creative Arts Management OÜ
All rights reserved.

Author: Juliana Wentworth
ISBN HARDBACK: 978-9916-90-076-5
ISBN PAPERBACK: 978-9916-90-077-2

Strands of Starlight Mysteries

In the depths of night's embrace,
Whispers of the cosmos trace.
Glimmers dance on velvet skies,
Secrets held where silence lies.

Celestial threads entwine so tight,
In shadows cast by pale moonlight.
Patterns weaved of dreams and fears,
Echoes of the past in tears.

The Celestial Embrace

Upon the horizon's gentle glow,
Stars awaken, soft and slow.
In the cradle of the night,
The universe holds its breath in sight.

With arms of light, it draws us near,
Whispers of love that we can hear.
In cosmic warmth, our souls entwine,
A dance of fate, celestial sign.

Ethereal Labyrinths

Wander through the misty paths,
Where shadows hide their silent laughs.
Every turn a secret kept,
In the labyrinth where dreams are swept.

Glistening lights through the dense grey,
Guide the heart, show the way.
Each corner turned reveals a face,
Of lost time and forgotten grace.

Luminescence of the Enigmatic

In twilight's glow, the unknown shines,
A tapestry of fate aligns.
Illusions weave in silken threads,
As beauty stirs where reason dreads.

Through the murk, a spark ignites,
Illuminates the hidden sights.
With every flicker, a story told,
Of mysteries in night so bold.

Sunsets of the Imagination

Colors blend in twilight's grace,
Dreams unfurl in quiet space.
Golden hues, a soft embrace,
Whispers dance in every place.

Clouds behave like flowing streams,
Carrying our secret dreams.
Each horizon softly gleams,
Painting life in vibrant themes.

The Lore of Starlit Journeys

Upon the path where starlight grows,
Adventure calls, the spirit knows.
Galaxies hum as the night flows,
In cosmic tales, the heart bestows.

Twinkling lights guide souls afar,
Through realms where wishes gently spar.
Each star a story, a hidden scar,
Binding us together from where we are.

Drifting Among Celestial Whispers

Silence wraps the cosmic night,
Whispers float, a soft delight.
Echoes of the stars take flight,
Drifting dreams to endless height.

Galactic winds weave through the dark,
Carrying secrets, a celestial spark.
Each breath a song, a quiet lark,
Connecting souls with gentle mark.

The Allure of Astral Visions

Visions swirl in starry streams,
Filling hearts with ancient dreams.
Galaxies dance, their light redeems,
In the night, hope brightly gleams.

Eyes closed tight, we drift and soar,
Through astral gates, forevermore.
In every pulse, in every lore,
The universe is our open door.

Whispers of Shadowed Shores

In twilight's calm, where shadows dance,
The whispers call, a soft romance.
Upon the sand, the secrets lay,
The tides recede, then come to play.

Moonlight glows on waters deep,
Where dreams and memories softly creep.
A story told by waves so near,
Of distant lands, held close and dear.

Shimmering Horizons of Wonder

Beyond the hills, where colors blend,
The sky unveils, horizons mend.
A tapestry of light and shade,
In every hue, a dream is laid.

The stars awaken, twinkling bright,
Each one a wish, a guiding light.
We chase the dawn with open hearts,
In every start, true magic sparks.

The Longing of the Cosmic Heart

In silent void, where echoes sway,
The cosmic heart beats night and day.
It seeks a soul to share its song,
To weave a tale, where dreams belong.

Through galaxies, its whispers roam,
In stardust paths, it yearns for home.
With every pulse, a spark ignites,
In the vast dark, love's light flights.

Echoes in the Veil of Space

In the stillness of the cosmic sea,
Echoes linger, wild and free.
From ancient stars, their voices call,
A symphony that binds us all.

Amid the void, tales come alive,
In the heart of night, dreams thrive.
Each echo holds a secret thought,
A universe where all are caught.

Celestial Elysium

In a realm where stars collide,
The whispers of the night reside.
Dreams take flight on moonlit beams,
Embracing light, unraveling dreams.

Through gardens kissed by cosmic grace,
Time unravels in this space.
Winds of starlight weave and twine,
In Elysium, all is divine.

Reflections in an Astral Pool

Beneath the sky of endless hue,
The water glimmers, bright and blue.
Stars dip low, their patterns swirl,
A dance of fate in cosmic whirl.

Each ripple holds a timeless tale,
Of distant worlds and cosmic sail.
Gaze within and you will find,
The universe's heart, entwined.

Wandering on the Edge of Infinity

Footsteps echo on the void,
In the silence, dreams enjoyed.
Galaxies drift in quiet grace,
In timeless realms, we find our place.

Thoughts like stardust gently flow,
Navigating paths we do not know.
On the edge, where shadows bend,
Infinity unfolds, no end.

Glimmers of the Unseen World

In hidden realms where spirits dwell,
Soft glimmers tell the tales they tell.
Whispers dance in twilight's haze,
   A symphony of ancient ways.

Through veils of light, we catch a glance,
Of mysteries held within a trance.
In shadows cast, the secrets fold,
   The unseen world forever bold.

Serene Wonders of the Infinite Sky

Beneath the wide and whispering blue,
Clouds drift like dreams, soft and true.
The sun dips low in a golden hue,
Painting the evening with a gentle view.

Stars awaken in the velvet night,
Each a beacon, glowing bright.
Moonlight dances, pure delight,
Embracing the world in its silver light.

A breeze carries secrets of old,
Stories of love and adventures bold.
Silhouettes of trees, graceful and cold,
Under the sky, so vast, so gold.

In tranquil moments, the heart finds peace,
As nature's beauty grants release.
In the sky's embrace, worries cease,
A realm where all can find their lease.

The Forgotten Wish of the Stars

Once upon a time, wishes soared,
Carried by comets, hopes adored.
In the silence of night, souls explored,
Seeking dreams that the heart restored.

Shadows of time linger in the air,
Whispers of wishes, both fragile and rare.
Stars twinkle softly, showing they care,
As laughter of children echoes everywhere.

Yet some wishes fade, lost and unseen,
Swallowed by darkness, a forgotten sheen.
Yet among the stars, pure and keen,
A wish still smiles, forever serene.

A reminder to dream, to never let go,
To seek out the light in the ebb and flow.
For every longing has room to grow,
In the heart of the night, let your spirits glow.

Celestial Journeys Unbound

Across the cosmos, dreams take flight,
On wings of stardust, through the night.
Galaxies swirling, a wondrous sight,
Infinite journeys, hearts alight.

Riding the waves of time and space,
Explorers of wonders in a timeless race.
Each twinkling star, a familiar face,
Guides our pathway through the celestial grace.

Nebulas bloom in vibrant hues,
Painting the skies with ethereal views.
Cosmic whispers, ancient clues,
In the vast unknown, we find new news.

With every heartbeat, the journey calls,
Into the vastness, where mystery sprawls.
In the embrace of the universe, love befalls,
Unbound and free, as starlight enthralls.

Dreams of the Starlit Sea

Whispers ride the ocean's breeze,
As waves dance under silver light.
In every curl, a secret tease,
A dreamer's heart ignites the night.

Beneath the gaze of twinkling stars,
The tides tell tales of love and loss.
Each ripple holds a memory's scars,
In salty depths, they softly cross.

Crafting worlds with every swell,
The sea sings songs of distant shores.
In this realm, our spirits dwell,
Where time drifts by and hope restores.

So let the waves embrace our fears,
In starlit waters, we shall soar.
With every heartbeat, fate appears,
And dreams of magic evermore.

Secrets Beneath the Ethereal Sky

Under the vast and endless dome,
Whispers float in the bittersweet air.
Hidden truths find their way home,
In shadows cast by starlight's glare.

The night reveals its gentle scheme,
With velvet hues and shimmering dust.
We chase our hopes, we chase a dream,
Within the sky, our souls entrust.

Every cloud, a storied drift,
Every star, a wish long cast.
In this vast space, our spirits lift,
As echoes of the past are grasped.

So linger here, where silence sings,
And secrets dance on twilight's sigh.
In the quiet, the heart takes wing,
Under the ethereal sky.

The Cradle of Forgotten Stars

In the cradle of ancient light,
Rest hidden worlds we used to know.
Forgotten dreams in endless night,
Where stardust whispers tales of woe.

The skies, a tapestry of fate,
Each twinkle hides a story old.
With every pulse, we contemplate,
The mysteries that stars have told.

In silence deep, we seek to find,
A spark of truth in cosmic grace.
The universe unfolds its mind,
As shadows weave through time and space.

So let us journey, hand in hand,
Through galaxies where hopes ignite.
In the embrace of twilight sand,
We'll find our way beneath the night.

Fables Woven in Moonlight

Underneath the silver glow,
Woven stories begin to dance.
Fables whispered soft and low,
In the night, our hearts entranced.

The moonlight weaves a magic thread,
A tapestry of dreams so bright.
Each tale told, a path we tread,
Guiding us through the veil of night.

Mysteries twirl in shadows' play,
As laughter echoes through the trees.
With every breath, we cease to stray,
In moonlit fables, the spirit frees.

So stay awhile in this embrace,
Where dreams collide and hopes ignite.
In the gentle glow, we find our place,
In fables woven in moonlight.

The Allure of Etheric Realities

In whispers soft, the shadows dance,
Where unseen realms begin to prance.
With every breath, a pulse of light,
Calling souls to take their flight.

The stars align in secret grace,
A mirrored gaze in time and space.
Mystic tides pull at the seams,
Awakening our latent dreams.

Veils of night and dawn's embrace,
Hold the truth of every place.
In ether's arms, we find our way,
Through realms where ancient spirits play.

Yet in this dance, we feel the pull,
Of what is known, yet beautiful.
To dive into the endless sea,
Of ether's vast eternity.

A Journey Through the Cosmic Mist

Amidst the stars where shadows weave,
A journey calls, yet we believe.
Through cosmic winds, we trail along,
To sing the universe's song.

Each step a spark that lights the night,
Guided by the moon's soft light.
The mist unfolds with each new breath,
A dance of life that conquers death.

Galaxies spin, a grand ballet,
Leading hearts that long to sway.
Through nebulas, our spirits soar,
To realms unknown, forevermore.

In silence deep, our hearts ignite,
With every pulse, we find the light.
In cosmic tides, we seek our bliss,
A journey born of love's sweet kiss.

The Symphony of the Celestial Winds

A symphony plays in the night's embrace,
With whispers of stars and endless space.
The winds that carry secrets untold,
Inspirations of the brave and bold.

From galaxies far, their echoes ring,
A song of hope that makes us sing.
Each note a spark, a stellar dream,
Floating softly on a cosmic stream.

In harmony, the worlds collide,
With music that flows like the turning tide.
Through each crescendo, hearts arise,
Underneath the vast, unending skies.

As etheric tunes sweep through our soul,
We find our place, and feel whole.
In every breath, the universe spins,
In the symphony of celestial winds.

Portraits of Forgotten Dreams

Upon the canvas of time's embrace,
Lie portraits of dreams, lost without trace.
Each brushstroke whispers tales of old,
Of hopes once bright, now muted gold.

In shadows deep, they softly glow,
Memories of what we used to know.
In faded hues, our dreams reside,
Awaiting the tides of time's low tide.

Yet in the heart, they stir and rise,
Like timeless echoes toward the skies.
Reviving wishes from years gone by,
With every sigh, we learn to fly.

So let us paint on life's vast field,
With colors bright, our fate revealed.
For in the portraits that we scheme,
Lies the magic of forgotten dreams.

The Alchemy of Enchanted Realms

In whispers of the night so deep,
Dreams weave magic, secrets keep.
Stars align, a dance divine,
In this realm, our hearts entwine.

Golden threads of fate are spun,
Beneath the moon, our journey's begun.
With every breath, the magic flows,
In enchanted realms, the wild wind blows.

Through forests dark, where shadows play,
Mystic creatures roam and sway.
The echo of laughter fills the air,
A spell of love, beyond compare.

Journey on, our spirits soar,
In the alchemy, we seek for more.
Hand in hand, through time we drift,
In these realms, our souls uplift.

When Shadows Sing to the Stars.

When shadows sing to the stars above,
The world transforms, lit by love.
Whispers carried on the breeze,
Nature's melody, hearts at ease.

Moonlit paths, where dreams take flight,
Dance of the shadows, soft and light.
Every twinkle, a tale to tell,
In the night, we cast our spell.

Through the silence, echoes soar,
Voices rise, forever more.
The night unfolds, revealing grace,
In this darkness, we find our place.

Embrace the whispers of the night,
As shadows sing, we feel the light.
Together, in this cosmic play,
When shadows sing, love finds its way.

Veils of Enchanted Light

Through veils of light, we find our way,
In twilight's touch, our dreams at play.
Golden hues in the morning dew,
Whispers of magic, soft and true.

Each step unfolds a hidden path,
Beneath the sky, we feel the math.
Stars align in a tranquil dance,
In the ether, our hearts entrance.

Beyond the veil, where visions weave,
In the fabric of time, we believe.
Secrets linger in the air,
In enchanted light, we cast our care.

With every heartbeat, the magic's near,
In veils of light, we lose our fear.
Together we wander, hand in hand,
In this mystical, radiant land.

Secrets of the Celestial Sea

In the depths of the celestial sea,
Secrets lie, waiting for thee.
Waves of stardust gently roll,
Whispers of truths, a cosmic soul.

Colors dance like dreams afloat,
In moonlit waters, we find our boat.
Navigating through time and space,
In the sea of love, we find our place.

With every wave, a story spins,
In the depths, where longing begins.
Eclipsed by time, our spirits rise,
In the celestial sea, where magic lies.

Catch the winds, let the currents flow,
In this ocean, our hearts will glow.
Together we'll sail, forever free,
Exploring the secrets of the sea.

Wanderscapes of Ethereal Beauty

In whispered winds, the flowers sway,
Beneath the light of the fading day.
Each petal sings of grace untold,
In colors bright and stories bold.

A river flows with silver gleam,
Reflecting softly a distant dream.
Where mountains touch the endless sky,
And clouds drift gently, floating high.

Among the trees, the shadows play,
Draped in hues of green and gray.
Nature's canvas, vast and wide,
Where secrets wait in quiet hide.

So wander through this tranquil land,
Each step a note, each breath a strand.
In wanderlust, let spirits soar,
In ethereal beauty, forevermore.

Chronicles of the Dreaming Sky

Beneath the veil of twilight's breath,
Stars awaken, defying death.
In whispers soft, the cosmos sighs,
Revealing tales from ancient skies.

The moon, a keeper of the night,
Casts silver shadows, pure and bright.
Each constellation holds a name,
In luminous light, their stories flame.

Clouds drift slow, like thoughts in mind,
Unraveling dreams we seek to find.
With every twinkling, wishes soar,
In echoes of the great folklore.

The nightingale sings her lullaby,
In reverence to the dreaming sky.
With every glance, our souls take flight,
In the chronicles of endless night.

Shadows on the Cosmic Canvas

Strokes of starlight paint the night,
A cosmic canvas, pure delight.
In vibrant hues, the dark unfolds,
A tapestry of stories bold.

Galaxies swirl with graceful spins,
Each spiral mirrors where life begins.
Nebulas bloom in colors bright,
A radiant dance in the tapestry of night.

Planets glide through the velvet space,
In silent whispers, they find their place.
Eclipses cast their fleeting shade,
On shadows where vast dreams are laid.

In this embrace, time flows and bends,
Where the ending and the start condescends.
A cosmic journey, infinite and grand,
In shadows cast by a creator's hand.

Tides of the Iridescent Night

Waves crash softly on the shore,
As night unfolds with a gentle roar.
The moon reflects on waters deep,
Where secrets linger, mysteries sleep.

Stars twinkle like pearls on the sea,
In the tides of night, wild and free.
Each ebb and flow tells a tale,
Of love and loss, of dreams that sail.

With every push and pull of the waves,
Hearts beat wildly, the spirit braves.
In shadows cast by an ocean's might,
We dance along the edge of night.

So let us wander, hand in hand,
Upon this iridescent strand.
Beneath the sky, so vast and bright,
We'll chase the tides of the dreaming night.

Whispers Beyond the Ether

In shadows cast by silent night,
The whispers flow, a soft delight.
Through realms unseen, they dance and weave,
A tapestry of what we believe.

Across the stars, the echoes play,
In cosmic winds, they drift away.
With every sigh, a story told,
Of secrets held in silence bold.

The moonlight glints on dreams untold,
And wraps the heart in threads of gold.
In quiet corners, thoughts align,
A gentle touch, a spark divine.

As night unfolds its velvet hue,
These whispers guide, they call to you.
In hushed tones, they beckon near,
To hear the fate we hold most dear.

Dreams in the Twilight Realm

In twilight's glow, where shadows play,
Dreams begin to drift away.
A world between the dusk and dawn,
Where hopes are born, and fears withdrawn.

The stars ignite, a distant song,
In harmony, they all belong.
With every breath, the night unfolds,
A canvas bright with tales retold.

Amidst the whispers of the trees,
Dreams flutter soft upon the breeze.
In this realm of twilight grace,
We find our peace, our sacred space.

As night descends, the magic flows,
In every heart, the longing grows.
To chase the dreams that softly gleam,
And wander far in twilight's dream.

The Enigma of Distant Shores

Upon the waves, a secret lies,
In distant shores beneath the skies.
With every tide that comes and goes,
The ocean breathes, the enigma flows.

A yearning heart, a sailor's song,
In search of where the souls belong.
The lighthouses call with guiding light,
To navigate the cloak of night.

Whispers carried on the breeze,
Of lands unseen, and tranquil seas.
With sails unfurled, we ride the storm,
In quest of shores where dreams are born.

The horizon stretches, wide and free,
Each wave a clue to destiny.
In silent depth, the secrets pour,
Unlock the mystery of the shore.

Luminous Pathways

In twilight's hue, the pathways glow,
With every step, the wonders flow.
Beneath the stars, where shadows light,
We wander forth into the night.

With lanterns bright, our spirits soar,
Illuminating what's in store.
The whispers lead, with gentle grace,
Towards the dreams that we embrace.

Each heartbeat counts, a rhythm true,
In luminous paths, we find the new.
With courage found in every thread,
We weave the stories yet unsaid.

So take my hand, let's walk this way,
Through vibrant nights to greet the day.
In pathways bright, our hearts entwine,
A dance of light, a love divine.

Tales from the Dreamer's Edge

In twilight whispers, shadows creep,
A world awakens, secrets deep.
The moonlight dances, casting spells,
Where every heartbeat, softly swells.

Eager souls, on paths unknown,
Embrace the magic, seeds are sown.
With every dream, new hopes arise,
A tapestry spun beneath the skies.

Guided by starlight's gentle hue,
They chase the visions that feel true.
In silent realms, their laughter weaves,
As time unravels, and heart believes.

Together they wander, hand in hand,
In lands untouched, where dreams expand.
These tales of wonder never cease,
Awakening souls, a timeless peace.

Dances of Darkened Wonder

In shadows deep, the spirits sway,
The night unfolds in soft ballet.
A haunting melody, whispered low,
Where every note ignites the glow.

The forest shivers, leaves take flight,
As ancient tales are born of night.
With every pulse, the darkness sings,
A symphony of secret things.

Beneath a canopy of stars,
They twirl, entwined, the lost memoirs.
In every curve, a story shines,
Each graceful step, a path defined.

Embrace the hush, the midnight air,
In dances spun, with elegant care.
For in this realm, where shadows play,
The darkened wonder lights the way.

Whirlwinds of Galactic Secrets

Stars collide in cosmic dance,
Galaxies whirl in a timeless trance.
In every twinkle, stories spun,
Whispers of worlds that were and are one.

Through stellar storms, the secrets hide,
In every pulse, the cosmos' pride.
Nebulas bright, in hues of fire,
Awakening dreams, igniting desire.

Voyagers bold, on starlit quests,
Seek knowledge deep, where wonder rests.
In patterns woven across the night,
They chase the echoes of ancient light.

With each new dawn, the mysteries bloom,
As swirling space unveils its room.
In this vast ocean, truths reside,
Galactic secrets—our hearts collide.

The Essence of Enchanted Skies

Upon the canvas, colors blend,
Whispers of magic, dreams transcend.
Clouds of silver, threads of gold,
In twilight's embrace, stories unfold.

The essence breathes in gentle breeze,
A lullaby sung through rustling leaves.
In playful hues, the sunset glows,
Painting the world in vivid shows.

Through mystic realms, the starlight streams,
Illuminating the heart's own dreams.
In this ballet of dusk and dawn,
A dance of life, where hope is drawn.

With every glance, the skies reveal,
A sacred bond, a timeless seal.
In the essence found, our spirits soar,
Enchanted skies forevermore.

Luminous Paths Through the Unknown

Faint glimmers guide the weary soul,
Beneath the stars, where shadows stroll.
Each step unfolds a story untold,
On paths of silver, a journey bold.

Whispers of dreams paint the night sky,
Inviting the lost to spread their wings high.
In the silence, a truth begins to shine,
Luminous paths through space and time.

With every heartbeat, the universe breathes,
Connecting the hearts that fate bequeathes.
In the dance of fate, we find our role,
Embracing the unknown, making us whole.

Future and past intertwine with grace,
Guiding us gently to a sacred place.
We walk through the darkness, yet feel the light,
Luminous paths, where dreams take flight.

Echoes of Ancient Light

In the hushed whispers of the night,
Ancient stories shimmer bright.
Crystals hum a forgotten lore,
Echoes of ages converge on the shore.

Stars weave tales of passion and strife,
Illuminating shadows, giving them life.
In the stillness, a heartbeat remains,
As time unfolds, the essence retains.

Lost civilizations in twilight's embrace,
Ghostly reflections, time won't erase.
Through the corridors of history, we tread,
Unraveling secrets in the words unsaid.

Every flicker births a new refrain,
A celestial melody that breaks the chain.
In the cosmic dance, we find our place,
Echoes of light, a timeless grace.

The Allure of the Veiled Realm

Beyond the veil, mysteries reside,
Elusive wonders we long to confide.
In the shadowed corners, magic breathes,
The allure of secrets, a heart that believes.

Whispers of dreams drift on the breeze,
Inviting adventurers, setting them at ease.
In hidden gardens, reality bends,
Luring the seekers, where the road ends.

Every glance reveals a story anew,
Colors blend softly into the blue.
The veiled realm beckons with a smile,
Promising treasures that last for a while.

In the twilight where worlds entwine,
The allure of the unseen, divine.
We walk on the edge of the known and unknown,
In the veiled realm, we find our home.

Veins of the Universe

In the cosmos, a rhythm pulses deep,
Veins of the universe, secrets they keep.
Flowing like rivers, stars intertwine,
Binding existence in a dance so fine.

Galaxies swirl, a cosmic embrace,
Each heartbeat resonates, a sacred space.
Woven together, we're part of this thread,
Veins of the universe, where all paths are led.

Time and light weave a tapestry grand,
Connecting us all, hand in hand.
In the vastness, we're never alone,
Veins of the universe, a shared home.

Beneath the heavens, we dream and aspire,
Igniting the spark of infinite fire.
With every breath, we honor the flow,
Veins of the universe, forever we glow.

Whispers of the Enchanted Dawn

In the hush of morning light,
Dreams awaken, taking flight.
Birds sing sweetly from the trees,
Carried softly on the breeze.

Golden rays begin to gleam,
Nature stirs; it feels like a dream.
Petals open, colors bloom,
Casting off the night's cold gloom.

Whispers linger, soft and bright,
Painting skies in pure delight.
The world anew, a canvas clear,
Embracing hope, dispelling fear.

Shadows Dance at the Edge of Twilight

In twilight's glow, the shadows sway,
Kissed by colors, gold and gray.
Whispers of night begin to creep,
As the weary world drifts to sleep.

Stars awaken, their watch begun,
In this dance beneath the sun.
Fading light, a gentle sigh,
As dreams begin to weave and fly.

Moonlight beckons, soft and clear,
As secrets murmur, drawing near.
In this hour, time stands still,
Beneath the stars, the heart can fill.

Celestial Veils Unfurled

Night unfurls its velvet hand,
Stars are scattered, bold and grand.
Whispers echo through the vast,
In cosmic dances, shadows cast.

Galaxies, in radiant swirl,
Guard the dreams in night's unfurl.
Mysterious paths, a glowing arc,
Guiding souls through the dark.

Each twinkle, a tale to tell,
Of lovers lost, of spirits fell.
Celestial winds begin to sing,
In the night, our hearts take wing.

Beyond the Veil of Dusk

Beneath the veil where shadows blend,
The day's warm laughter starts to end.
Colors blend, a fading song,
In this magic, we all belong.

The sky a canvas, deep and wide,
Holds the secrets that we hide.
Moments linger, soft and deep,
As the world begins to sleep.

Beneath the stars, our stories soar,
In whispered dreams forevermore.
Beyond the dusk, we find our way,
Into the night, where wishes stay.

The Siren's Call from Beyond the Mists

Whispers echo through the night,
Calling sailors lost in plight.
Voices weave a spell so deep,
Luring hearts that yearn to leap.

Mists envelop the ghostly tide,
Guiding souls where shadows hide.
Songs of longing, sharp like knives,
In the depths, the siren thrives.

Each note wraps around the mind,
In the fog, no peace to find.
Promises of love and grace,
Yet danger lurks in every trace.

In the dark where spirits weep,
A haunting call that pulls the sleep.
Tempting hearts to sail so far,
To follow lights, a distant star.

Embrace of the Elusive Dawn

Softly breaks the light of day,
Chasing shadows, paving way.
Colors blend with gentle grace,
Nature's calm, a warm embrace.

In the hush before the sound,
Hope and dreams are tightly bound.
Birds begin their morning song,
In the glow, we all belong.

Rays of light start to unfold,
Stories of the night retold.
Each new moment, fresh and bright,
Painting skies with golden light.

As the dawn begins to rise,
Awakening the sleepy skies.
Feel the warmth upon your face,
In this moment, find your place.

Stars Speak to the Silent

In the silence of the night,
Stars above are shining bright.
Whispers travel through the dark,
Little sparks ignite the spark.

Lonely hearts gaze up in awe,
Searching skies for signs they saw.
Stories whispered on the breeze,
Carried far across the seas.

Messages from worlds untold,
Ancient dreams in silver gold.
Each constellation bears a tale,
In the dark, their voices sail.

Listen close, let silence reign,
Hear the echoes, feel the pain.
Stars connect us, heart to heart,
In their light, we're never far.

A Tapestry of Ether and Dreams

Weaving threads of night and day,
In the realms where dreams hold sway.
Colors dance in waltzing flight,
Painting visions into night.

Layers blend in cosmic streams,
Crafted softly from our dreams.
Nebulas drift, so vast, so wide,
In this place, our hopes abide.

Fading echoes softly hum,
Whispers of what's yet to come.
Each connection, fragile spun,
Threads of fate, we're all as one.

In this tapestry so grand,
We find solace, hand in hand.
Ethereal paths of light and shade,
In dreams' embrace, we are remade.

Shadowed Realms of Wonder

In twilight's grip, the whispers weave,
Of dreamers lost, their hearts believe.
Beneath the stars, the secrets bloom,
In shadowed realms, the night consumes.

With every step, the echoes call,
To hidden paths where shadows fall.
A dance of light, a flicker's game,
In wonder's realm, we seek the flame.

The twilight mist holds tales untold,
Of ancient beings, brave and bold.
In tangled woods where shadows play,
The heart shall find its secret way.

So wander forth, with courage bright,
Embrace the dream, the realm of night.
For in the dark, the light will gleam,
In shadowed realms, we dare to dream.

Fables of the Otherworld

In whispers soft, fables arise,
From realms where time and magic tie.
With every word, a story spun,
Of battles lost and victories won.

From enchanted glades and misty halls,
The echoes of their laughter calls.
In twilight's glow, they sing their songs,
Where every heart and spirit belongs.

On golden shores where spirits roam,
They craft their tales, a timeless home.
In twilight shades, the truth entwines,
In fables told, the heart aligns.

So gather close, let magic flow,
In otherworld, where wonders grow.
For in each tale, a spark ignites,
Fables of dreams and endless nights.

The Hidden Tapestry of Time

In woven threads, the past resides,
A tapestry where truth abides.
Each stitch a story, bright and bold,
Of moments lost, yet to be told.

From days of yore to futures bright,
The fabric glows with whispered light.
In every fold, a secret sways,
In hidden time, the heart displays.

The clock unwinds, the fibers weave,
In every breath, we dare believe.
For time's embrace is tender, kind,
In hidden paths, our souls will find.

So journey forth, through strands of fate,
Where each moment is a golden gate.
The tapestry reveals its design,
In hidden realms, a truth divine.

Navigating Through Celestial Currents

In cosmic seas where stardust swirls,
We chart our course through vast, bright pearls.
With every heartbeat, galaxies gleam,
Navigating through a cosmic dream.

Upon the winds of heavenly flow,
We seek the paths where wishes go.
In serene silence, the planets spin,
In celestial currents, we begin.

The universe sings a timeless song,
In harmony where we belong.
With each star's light, our spirits rise,
In navigating the endless skies.

So take my hand, let's drift away,
With every breath, we seize the day.
In cosmic dance, our souls unite,
Through celestial currents, we find light.

Illuminated Pathways of the Arcane

In shadows deep, the whispers dwell,
Mysteries bound in a timeless spell.
With lanterns bright, we tread the night,
Guided forth by flickering light.

The air is thick with ancient lore,
As echoes dance on the spectral floor.
In every turn, a secret wakes,
The heart uncovers what silence makes.

Through emerald woods and silver streams,
We wander lost in forgotten dreams.
The arcane path unfolds in grace,
A journey bold we must embrace.

With minds alight, our spirits soar,
To realms unknown, forevermore.
Under stars that brightly gleam,
We trace the line of a waking dream.

A Voyage Through Time's Veil

Set sail across the timeless sea,
Where moments swirl like memory.
With sails aloft, the winds align,
To guide us forth through the edge of time.

The stars above, a charted course,
Whispering tales of a hidden force.
Each wave that breaks, a story spun,
A dance of days, now lost, now won.

In every tide, our futures blend,
Past and present, forever send.
The horizon blurs, as shadows bend,
In time's embrace, we find our friends.

Amidst the storms, the calm we seek,
Through echoes faint, our hearts will speak.
In unity, we drift, we glide,
On time's vast ocean, side by side.

Secrets Entwined in Light

In dawn's embrace, the shadows flee,
Revealing truths for eyes to see.
With every ray, a thought ignites,
A tapestry of hidden sights.

Beneath the veil of morning mist,
Lies a world that we can't resist.
Each secret wrapped in glowing hue,
Unfolds the path to something new.

In whispers soft, the stories play,
As golden beams chase dark away.
The light reveals what darkness hides,
In harmony where love abides.

Together we explore the dawn,
Entwined in light, forever drawn.
A dance of hope, a sacred trust,
In secrets pure, we learn to adjust.

The Embrace of the Celestial Veil

Above the world, the stars ignite,
A canvas spun in the fabric of night.
Each twinkling gem, a distant call,
In the embrace of the universe, we fall.

Galaxies swirl in an endless dance,
Inviting us to join the trance.
With hearts aflame, we reach in prayer,
To touch the veil of the cosmic air.

In tranquil silence, the cosmos speaks,
Each heartbeat echoes, the soul it seeks.
In the vast expanse, we find our place,
A gentle hug in the eternal space.

So let us wander, hand in hand,
Through stardust paths, a wonderland.
In the embrace of a celestial night,
We share our dreams in the endless light.

The Unseen Footprints of Fate

In shadows cast by whispered dreams,
Fate walks quietly, or so it seems.
Each step a mark, yet none can see,
The paths we tread, where we might be.

Moments blend like colors bright,
A tapestry woven in the night.
With every choice, the story bends,
A journey where no wandering ends.

Beneath the stars, we feel the pull,
Of destinies vast, yet so small.
Guided by the unseen threads,
Where hearts lead on, the mind dreads.

In silence echoes a gentle call,
Which binds us tight, we rise, we fall.
So trust the dance of chance, my friend,
For every start is a welcomed end.

Radiance of the Hidden Depths

Beneath the calm of azure skies,
Lie secrets whispered, soft, discrete lies.
Hidden depths that shimmer bright,
Awaiting souls to find their light.

In every heart a story waits,
A spark within that elevates.
Dare to descend, unearth the glow,
Where shadows played, let wonder flow.

In silence deep, a voice so clear,
Calls out to those who dare to steer.
Through tangled roots, we plunge, explore,
To find the treasures, forevermore.

With every dive, we lose the fear,
And find the light that waits so near.
For in the dark, we rise anew,
With radiant hearts, we journey through.

Chasing Whirlwinds of the Soul

On tempest winds, our spirits soar,
Through unseen realms, we seek for more.
In dizzy dance, our dreams take flight,
Chasing whispers of the night.

Round and round, the chaos spins,
In every loss, a chance that wins.
With open hearts, we chase the breeze,
Embracing change with graceful ease.

Surrendered now to the unseen flow,
Where every gust brings truth to show.
We'll ride the storms, with passions bold,
For in the whirlwinds, life unfolds.

So hold my hand, let's take the leap,
Into the unknown, our spirits deep.
Together we'll chase what life bestows,
In whirlwind dance, our journey grows.

Threads of Destiny in Velvet Night

In velvet night, the stars align,
Weaving destinies, yours and mine.
Each thread of fate, so fine and rare,
Entwined together, beyond compare.

With every heartbeat, stories weave,
A fabric rich, in dreams believe.
Under the moon's soft, guiding light,
We find our place in the cosmic flight.

Gentle whispers, a call so sweet,
We follow paths where shadows meet.
Threads pulled taut, yet freely spun,
In this grand tale, we are but one.

So let us dance, beneath the glow,
Of countless stars, that softly show.
In velvet night, our spirits rise,
Bound by the threads that never die.

Castles of Clouded Whispers

In twilight's soft embrace, they rise,
With towers made of dreamlit sighs.
Veils of mist wrap secrets tight,
Holding shadows in the night.

Glimmers dance on azure streams,
Where reality gently seams.
Echoes linger, tales unsaid,
In these castles, hopes are fed.

Lost within the silver haze,
We wander through the whispered maze.
Every breeze a phantom's breath,
Carrying stories of life and death.

Yet in the quiet, solace dwells,
In every corner, magic swells.
Castles wait for hearts to find,
The gentle whispers intertwined.

The Unseen Dance of Realms

Behind the veil of daily grind,
Lies a waltz of threads entwined.
Realms collide in soft ballet,
Where shadows lead, and visions play.

Stars align in silence deep,
Awakening dreams from slumbered sleep.
A tapestry of colors bloom,
In twilight's gentle, drawing room.

Veils flutter as the breezes weave,
Mysteries that hearts believe.
Each moment a step, a chance to sway,
In the unseen dance, we find our way.

Lift your gaze, let spirits twirl,
In this magic, let life unfurl.
For realms unseen through eyes remain,
Yet in our hearts, they leave their stain.

Constellations of Quietude

In the stillness of the night,
Stars whisper tales in lucent light.
Each flicker holds a sigh, a dream,
In constellations, we find our theme.

Silent realms where hearts can rest,
In cosmic patterns, we are blessed.
Floating through the velvet blue,
Time stands still, as if it knew.

Galaxies of peace arise,
In every shimmer, hope complies.
A soft embrace from worlds above,
We gather echoes filled with love.

Rest your fears beneath the sky,
Let the stars breathe lullabies.
For in each quiet, glowing hue,
Constellations cradle me and you.

The Great Beyond Beckons

Beyond the hills, where shadows fade,
A call persists, a serenade.
Winds of change whisper and sway,
The great beyond invites to play.

Golden rays pierce morning's mist,
With every pulse, a dream persists.
Paths untraveled in light traverse,
In the unknown, we find our verse.

Every heartbeat, a step anew,
Ventures await, calling the few.
From valleys deep to mountains high,
The great beyond unveils the sky.

Take a breath, let courage steer,
In the cosmic dance, have no fear.
For the journey flows, a vast expanse,
Into the great beyond, we dance.

Wandering the Twilight Passage

In twilight's gaze, I tread the path,
Whispers of night, a gentle breath.
Stars above, like distant dreams,
Guide my heart through silver streams.

Each shadow sways, a dance so light,
Moonbeams weave through the veil of night.
Footsteps soft on a carpet of dew,
Every moment feels both old and new.

The horizon blurs, a painted sky,
Where secrets linger and echoes lie.
With open arms, the night unfolds,
In its embrace, my spirit molds.

Wandering forth, the dark I greet,
Finding solace on this quiet street.
As time ebbs, I chase the glow,
Of twilight's kiss, where dreamers go.

The Convergence of Starry Dreams

Beneath the arch of shimmering stars,
Dreams collide, no matter how far.
Ethereal whispers call my name,
In this dance, I feel no shame.

Constellations map a sacred space,
Where wishes linger, a soft embrace.
A tapestry of hopes enshrined,
In every heartbeat, fate aligned.

Twinkling eyes in night's vast dome,
Invite my soul to wander home.
Through cosmic threads, our fates are tied,
In this ballet, with stars as guide.

Together we rise, like dawn's first light,
Igniting dreams that take to flight.
In the convergence of dreams we soar,
And find a world worth longing for.

The Ethereal Gateway

Beyond the mist, a portal glows,
An entrance where the dreamer goes.
With trembling hands, I reach inside,
To face the worlds where wonders hide.

Echoes dance in the twilight sheen,
A realm unseen, yet felt, serene.
Ghostly pathways stretch and wind,
To places only hearts can find.

Through the gateway, time stands still,
Imagination whispers, strong as will.
Each step a chance, each breath a song,
In this sanctuary, I belong.

Colors swirl in a vibrant crest,
Where souls can meet and hearts can rest.
With every heartbeat, secrets flow,
In the ethereal space, where dreams grow.

Shadows of Wistful Fantasies

In shadows deep, where dreams take flight,
Wistful fantasies emerge from night.
Silhouettes of hopes, softly tread,
In the quiet whispers, softly said.

Echoes of laughter twirl like smoke,
Fleeting moments, a tender cloak.
Between the worlds of what could be,
Shadows dance, longing to be free.

The heart remembers every trace,
Of fleeting dreams and time's embrace.
With echoes gentle, they weave and spin,
In the tapestry of where we've been.

In dusk's tender grasp, we find our way,
Through shadows cast by the light of day.
Each fantasy whispers a truth we share,
In the depths of longing, we find our prayer.

The Call of Phantom Skylines

In the mist where shadows play,
Cities whisper from far away,
With towers that reach for a hidden light,
Eclipsed secrets of the night.

Voices echo through the air,
Inviting dreams beyond compare,
To wander paths we've yet to roam,
Finding in silence a kindred home.

Time stands still, a gentle pause,
As visions beckon without cause,
Lost in echoes, spirits soar,
Chasing wonders forevermore.

Beneath the stars, a phantom guide,
Leads the heart where hopes reside,
In the realm of what could be,
Awakening souls to set them free.

Whims of the Uncharted

In lands where maps fade into dreams,
Nature's voice sings in gentle streams,
With laughter carried by the breeze,
And secrets hidden in the trees.

Waves of wildflowers dance and sway,
While shadows mingle at the end of day,
Each footstep whispers tales of old,
Of daring hearts and spirits bold.

Between the earth and sky so vast,
The future mingles with the past,
Adventures wait in every sigh,
Underneath the endless sky.

Bold explorers leave their mark,
As night descends and ignites the spark,
With stars as compass, they will find,
The whims of fate, both fierce and kind.

Beyond the Horizon's Secret

The sun dips low, a golden hue,
As dreams unfurl in skies so blue,
Each wave a promise on the shore,
Of whispered secrets, wanting more.

The horizon calls with open arms,
A siren song of ancient charms,
With every step, the heart beats fast,
In search of shadows from the past.

Mountains loom with tales untold,
In whispers soft, they still behold,
The echoes of those who dared to roam,
Across the land, away from home.

What lies beyond, we cannot see,
Yet still, we chase eternity,
In twilight's glow, a shimmer bright,
Awakens dreams and sparks delight.

Silhouettes of Forgotten Lore

In the quiet hush of fading light,
Silhouettes dance in the coming night,
Figures etched in the twilight's grace,
Whispers of time, a sacred space.

Beneath the stars, old stories dwell,
Echoes of laughter, a distant bell,
With every shadow, wisdom flows,
In the silence, the heart still knows.

Forgotten tales on the breeze are blown,
In every heart a seed is sown,
Of legends spun from dreams once shared,
At twilight's gate, the soul is bared.

So listen close to the night's embrace,
For in each shadow, we find our place,
In silhouettes, the past returns,
As history whispers, the spirit learns.

Where Time Bends in Silence

In quiet corners, shadows play,
With whispers lost in twilight's sway.
The hours fold, an unseen thread,
Where memories linger, softly spread.

Echoes dance in muted grace,
As stillness weaves a timeless space.
A gentle sigh, a breath, a hush,
In silence, time begins to blush.

Ancient trees with wisdom stand,
Roots entwined in fertile land.
Moments turn like whispered dreams,
In the silence, all is as it seems.

So let us gaze into the night,
Where time bends low and stars ignite.
In this embrace, we find our way,
Through silent hours, we drift and sway.

The Flight of Phantom Harbingers

Upon the wind, the whispers glide,
With wings of night, they softly bide.
Phantoms pull at strings unseen,
In twilight's realm, where dreams convene.

Silent calls from shadows deep,
In the dark, the echoes creep.
They paint the sky with secrets rare,
In flight, they vanish from our care.

Beacons flicker, guiding eyes,
Through spectral paths, under starlit skies.
A dance of fate, a fleeting trace,
The harbingers of time and space.

So let us watch the specters soar,
In the stillness, we seek for more.
With every flutter, they remind,
Of dreams that linger, unconfined.

Nebula's Lament at the Break of Day

In cosmic hues, the darkness weeps,
As dawn awakens, softly creeps.
Nebula's heart, a shimmering sigh,
Cradles the stars as they slip by.

Lost in the folds of endless night,
Celestial echoes, pure delight.
Each tear a star, a memory bright,
In the embrace of morning light.

A tapestry of dreams once spun,
In silence, morn greets the sun.
Cosmic whispers fade away,
In the arms of a brand new day.

The nebula's tale, a gentle ache,
Of love and loss, the dreams we make.
Through every breath, we learn to stay,
As night flows into light's ballet.

Portals in the Gossamer Air

In whispers thin, the edges blur,
Where fantasies and wishes stir.
Portals open with a gentle sigh,
To realms beyond, where spirits fly.

Threads of light in gossamer weave,
Drawing hearts that long to believe.
Curiosity waits beyond the veil,
In shimmering paths where dreams prevail.

Through the mists, adventure calls,
Behind each doorway, wonder sprawls.
Veils of time and space intertwine,
In the air, a hint divine.

So take a step, embrace the dare,
And wander through the magic air.
For in these portals, life renews,
A dance of dreams in vibrant hues.

Echoes of the Unknown

Whispers in the dark, a call so near,
Footsteps on the path, yet no one here.
Shadows twist and turn, secrets unfold,
In the silent night, mysteries told.

The moonlight glimmers, a soft embrace,
Through the veil of night, we find our place.
Echoes of the past linger and sigh,
In this quiet realm, we learn to fly.

Voices of ages, ancient and wise,
Guide us through dreamscapes, vast and wide.
Through whispers of memory, we roam,
Finding in the dark, a heart to call home.

Beyond the horizon, a flicker of hope,
In the shadows cast, we learn to cope.
For every echo that beckons in flight,
Leads us to the dawn, breaking the night.

A Dance with Starlit Shadows

In the twilight glow, shadows entwine,
Beneath the stars, their patterns align.
We sway with the breeze, bodies in tune,
Dancing with shadows, under the moon.

Their whispers call out, secrets replete,
In this cosmic ball, our worlds meet.
Footsteps of light on the velvet sky,
Captured in stardust, we leap and fly.

Echoing laughter, a celestial song,
In this astral moment, we both belong.
With every turn, our spirits ignite,
A dance with the shadows, a tapestry of light.

As the night deepens, we hold the sway,
In the heart of the cosmos, we lose our way.
Yet in this embrace, forever we stay,
A dance with starlit shadows, come what may.

The Veil of Cosmic Dreams

In a realm unseen, where visions fly,
The veil of dreams whispers a gentle sigh.
Stars weave together, stories unfold,
Through cosmic threads, destinies told.

Floating on wishes, we drift and roam,
In the universe vast, we call it home.
Fragments of time, a spectral delight,
Caught in the web of the starlit night.

Celestial wonders, shimmering bright,
Give life to our dreams, take flight from the night.
The veil lifts softly, inviting our gaze,
Into the embrace of infinite ways.

Here in the silence, we learn to believe,
In the magic of dreams, we dare to achieve.
Under cosmic skies, our hearts intertwined,
The veil of our visions, forever aligned.

Wanderers in the Nebula

Lost in the clouds of shimmering light,
Wanderers drift, guided by night.
Nebula's embrace, tender and bold,
In these swirling mists, our stories unfold.

Stars upon stars, a celestial sea,
We dance through the cosmos, wild and free.
Exploring the wonders, both strange and grand,
In the heart of the nebula, hand in hand.

Time ebbs and flows in this vast expanse,
Every heartbeat a provocative dance.
Through galaxies bright, our spirits convene,
Wanderers we are, in this haunting dream.

As colors collide in a vibrant display,
We lose ourselves in the beauty of play.
In the depths of the stars, forever we roam,
Wanderers in the nebula, finding our home.

Beyond the Boundless Skies

Above the clouds, where eagles soar,
Dreams are born, forevermore.
In colors bright, the sunsets blend,
Whispers of hope that never end.

Winds of change begin to blow,
Guiding hearts to where they grow.
In silent nights, the stars align,
With every wish, the soul will shine.

Mountains high and valleys deep,
In nature's arms, the secrets keep.
A tapestry of life unfolds,
With stories rich that time beholds.

Beyond the boundless skies, we roam,
In every heart, we find a home.
Each journey taken, leaves a trace,
In the heavens, we find our place.

The Portal of Quiet Reverie

In shadows soft, where silence breathes,
A portal opens, nature weaves.
Moments pause, the world stands still,
In this embrace, we drink our fill.

Gentle echoes of a tender thought,
In whispered dreams, joy's net is caught.
With every sigh, the heart will dance,
In quiet realms, we find our chance.

Reflections deep in tranquil streams,
Reality fades into our dreams.
Through tangled paths of mind we glide,
In reverie's arms, we will reside.

The stars will guide, the moon will sway,
In quietude, we find our way.
Every heartbeat, soft as dew,
In this stillness, I find you.

Threads of the Universe

In cosmic strands, much more than light,
Weaving tales both day and night.
Galaxies dance in the expanse wide,
In patterns deep where wonders hide.

Every star, a whispered dream,
In the tapestry, we find our theme.
Across the sky, our stories thread,
Binding all in the paths we tread.

From ancient roots to future skies,
The universe breathes, and love complies.
In the chaos, a symphony's found,
With every heartbeat, the world goes round.

So let us walk this starlit path,
Embracing joy, escaping wrath.
Together we weave, our destinies,
In threads of hope, the universe frees.

Secrets in the Starlight

Underneath the velvet night,
The stars reveal their softest light.
In their glow, old stories gleam,
Secrets whispered, like a dream.

Nebulas swirl in a cosmic dance,
Inviting souls to take a chance.
In every twinkle, love resides,
While the universe carefully hides.

Galactic winds sweep through our hearts,
Unfolding truths that time imparts.
In stardust trails, our hopes ignite,
Filling the void with pure delight.

So let us gaze at the heavens near,
With every secret, we draw close, dear.
In the starlight, our souls will soar,
Finding whispers forevermore.

Beyond the Twilight Gleam

The daylight fades, colors blend,
Shadows stretch where whispers tend.
Stars awaken in the azure dome,
A promise of the night to roam.

Gentle breezes dance and sway,
Carrying the secrets of the day.
Moonlight spills on tranquil streams,
Painting visions, weaving dreams.

In silence deep, the world holds breath,
As twilight whispers tales of depth.
Each star a spark, a distant guide,
Leading hearts where wonders bide.

Beyond the gleam, the heart takes flight,
In the embrace of the velvet night.
Boundless realms wait to be explored,
In the twilight, our spirits soared.

The Last Breath of the Celestial Night

As dark descends, the stars ignite,
A final sigh, the end of light.
The cosmos breathes in silent grace,
A fleeting moment, time can't replace.

The moon hangs low, a watchful eye,
Over dreams that drift and fly.
In the stillness, wishes blend,
Yearning for dawn, with none to fend.

Nebulas swirl in vibrant hues,
Secrets hidden in the views.
The galaxies hum their ancient tune,
A lullaby 'neath the silver moon.

Yet dawn will break, the shadows flee,
Rebirth awaits in harmony.
For every night, a promise made,
In morning's glow, all fears will fade.

Unraveling the Fabric of Infinity

Threads of starlight intertwine,
Across the cosmos, silent, divine.
Each point of light, a story spun,
In the loom of time, we are one.

Galaxies whisper, secrets unfold,
A tapestry of dreams retold.
In every heartbeat, echoes soar,
The pulse of life, forevermore.

The universe sings in tranquil waves,
A symphony for the lost and brave.
In the void, hope lights the way,
Guiding souls who dare to stay.

In mysteries deep, we find our place,
Infinity's dance, a timeless grace.
With each discovery, we embrace
The boundless love of time and space.

Conversations with the Cosmic Winds

Through the silence, whispers flow,
Carried softly, secrets grow.
The cosmic winds, they weave and spin,
Echoes of where we've always been.

They sing of worlds beyond our sight,
Of distant stars, in velvet night.
With every sigh, the heavens speak,
In gentle tones, though words are weak.

Riding currents of the unknown,
We feel the pulse, the thirst, the bone.
Each breath, a bridge to realms anew,
Conversations with the sky so blue.

As we listen, hearts align,
With the rhythms of the divine.
In fleeting moments, wisdom flows,
In cosmic winds, our true self grows.

The Transience of Celestial Echoes

Stars flicker in a velvet sky,
Whispers of time drift softly by.
Moments painted in silver light,
Fleeting glimpses of a cosmic night.

Planets waltz in orbits grand,
Tracing paths written in sand.
Eclipses fade with dawn's embrace,
Leaving shadows in empty space.

Comets flare and then are lost,
Scattered dreams at a hidden cost.
In silence, galaxies expand,
While echoes drift in a cosmic band.

Each heartbeat a luminous sigh,
An echo of wishes that never die.
Yet in the night, they slowly wane,
Celestial songs bearing joy and pain.

Murmurs from the Astral Sea

Waves of starlight gently flow,
Carrying tales of long ago.
In the depths, the secrets dwell,
Singing softly, a wistful shell.

Nebulas swirl in colors rare,
Painting stories in the air.
A tapestry of dreams untold,
Whispered wishes, bright and bold.

Comets race through in silent glee,
While galaxies sway in harmony.
The tide of time washes ashore,
A cosmic rhythm forevermore.

Listen close to the cosmic hum,
A lullaby from the stars to come.
Each twinkle, a note in the vast sea,
Murmurs of love and eternity.

Glowing Threads of Infinity

Weaving through the tapestry bright,
Threads of time shimmer in flight.
Interwoven tales of fate,
Boundless patterns we create.

In the loom of night, we string,
Galactic dreams on silken wing.
Each stitch a wish, each knot a sigh,
In the fabric where stars lie.

Constellations guide our way,
Marker of night, keeper of day.
With every glimmer, paths align,
Our destinies in designs divine.

In this dance of endless space,
We find our dreams, we trace our grace.
Through radiant nights, let love transcend,
Threads of infinity, without end.

Enchantment in the Ether

In the hush of cosmic grace,
Magic lingers in every space.
Whispers drift like softest sighs,
Enchantment weaves beneath the skies.

Stars ignite with timeless glow,
Casting spells that ebb and flow.
A ballet of dreams, a celestial play,
Guiding our hearts, lighting the way.

In the ether, wonders bloom,
Filling emptiness with sweet perfume.
Every twinkle, a sorcerer's art,
A sprinkle of stardust on the heart.

Each night an omen, each dawn reborn,
The magic of life in silence worn.
In every breath, the universe sings,
Enchanting hearts with infinite wings.

Milton Keynes UK
Ingram Content Group UK Ltd.
UKHW022050111124
451035UK00014B/1032